www.foreverhappylife.com

HAPPINESS LIFE

Your Simple Proven 3 Step Guide to Making Radical Self-Improvement Today book

(Motivational, Self-Help, Personal Growth & Inspirational)

the basics book #1

Jimmy J. Johnson

RoyceCardiff
Publishing House

Copyright © 2012

Forth-Edition

Paperback ISBN-13: 978-0615940489

Paperback ISBN-10: 061594048X

Digital Format ASIN: B00B0U9VEA

Printed in the United States of America
JimmyJeromeJohnson@gmail.com

Photo credits: Author, friends and Richard Sullivan

INTRODUCTION

I was born on the wrong side of the train tracks in Detroit, Michigan, USA; my father; when he was younger; actually lived in a government housing project. My family was a typical dysfunctional mess. I had no formal education other than high school. I worked hard to create a good income for myself. I bought many toys, the usual houses, cars, boats, planes and some bling and so on and so on. Oh yes, and the beautiful girls! Sometimes I was so depressed I didn't want to get out of bed or I would binge on food, alcohol or overindulge in other activities detrimental to my well-being. I never had a relationship that lasted over three years. I had this big hole that I could not fill. All the stuff and the three wives (one at a time of course) did not make me happy. What was life about? So I invested over 30 years, thousands of hours and enough cash to buy small retirement home in Florida in which to study many religions, self-improvement products, hundreds of books and anything I thought would help. I got to spend some time with some amazing people—just to name a few: Tony Robbins(Life Coach), Robert Kiyosaki(Rich Dad Poor Dad), Shawn Phillips(Body for Life), Bob Proctor(Life and Business coach). I even meditated with the Dalai Lama! Very cool!

What has been the benefit? Doctors say I have a body much younger than my age; true love, I'm with an amazing woman and proud to call her my wife and friend (she smiles a lot even when she sleeps); and I have a marvelous daughter, who teaches me something new every day. We live in a tropical paradise minutes from some of the finest beaches in the world. Also, with just a few hours' flight we can be in some of the most fascinating exotic countries. I choose to work from my house on my schedule. I have time and resources to spend with friends and family around the globe. Currently I have been to 18 countries and counting. That is all well and good, but the bigger thing is how I feel. I'm not saying life is a hundred percent perfect. But it is pretty close. If you could just spend one day with me you would understand. Life is good!

I'm not mentioning this to brag. I'm saying this to impress something upon you. I want you to understand where I came from and what I went through: I made and lost millions, I had huge emotional losses and no real family for support. And to top it off the doctors told me I had bipolar disorder at the age of 21 and should be on drugs for the rest of my life.

So my point is if you want to see some change, I mean amazing changes in your life—for example incredible friendships, blissful happiness continually, more money and amazing health—you can definitely learn something from this book series and you can do it.

If I can totally turn my life around from where I came from, then I know you can do better than me!

Imagine yourself happy like never before! This little book has made a huge difference for so many people, so at the end of this book I will ask you for a review, that way others can find it and benefit from it also.

Before you review it though, you have to read it :-)

So—let's get started.

Wishing you more love and happiness,

World traveler, adventurer and entrepreneur

Jimmy Jerome Johnson

TABLE OF CONTENTS

CHAPTER 1

FOREVER HAPPY LIFE
SELF-COMPASSION

The reason why this book came about is that I see so many people in the world who could be even happier; many of them have great ups and downs and big events, are very happy for a period of time, and then they crash. I have seen the same outrageous joy in my life, only to be followed later by a deep depression and a lot of self-loathing. Damn, that sucked.

I've had the good fortune of being able to invest a small fortune and thousands of hours studying self-improvement and religion through books, tapes, DVDs, seminar classes, retreats, consulting with gurus, and so on. I have spent time with many experts in many fields of extreme self-improvement and spiritually centered practices. For example, Time with Hot Coals Walker, Tony Robbins, and Hugging Trees Naked with Native Americans! From Buddhist to Baptists! I went on two different ten-day retreats without speaking, ate vegetarian and meditated five to six hours per day! I've stayed in a multitude of locations, from sleeping on a cement bed with a wooden pillow to luxury hotels with top self-help gurus at $4000 per weekend. I have not done it all; however, I have done enough.

I have seen that many people do not see the big picture. They seem to know nothing about happiness; they don't understand that they have control over their own being. Many of the teachings around the world can get you to the door of greater happiness.

However, it is your job, and only your job, to open that door. If you do the correct things, it need not be difficult. Also, it need not take a long time. I have met a few people who have spent their whole lives seeking the truth. I met a 70-year-old English monk who had spent four hours a day meditating and more than 40 years behind the walls of monasteries. He seemed to me to be one of the most unhappy persons I've ever met; it was very easy to see in his dropping wax like face. I'm going to show you, in this book, how, in a very short time (as quickly as twenty-four hours), you can have much more happiness in your life, and how to keep that happiness.

I retired at the age of 47, healthy, happy, and madly in love! I live in a very beautiful place and have an amazing lifestyle. I am very successful by most people's standards. What did I learn and how will it benefit you? I spent countless hours working on myself. Were some of the things I paid a lot of money for worthless, a waste of time, and just plain junk? Yes, many things were and I will save you the heartache of going through that. Did all this educational stuff help me? Yes, of course! Is the information new and revolutionary? The information found in my book is what I have learned from great teachers, sages, poets, ministers, monks, and drunks; my personal observations and life itself. If you have done a lot of personal self-development, it's possible some of this is not new to you (except maybe for Chapter 7, the **ZONE**), however, it may be of great benefit to you as a simple reminder of what works and how to get there simpler and quicker. If you're new to self-development, this simple information will change the way you see everything. It's possible to go through many paradigm shifts, like peeling the layers of an onion. The good news is many of these of educational programs were fantastic and I had many paradigm shifts throughout the years. You do not need to spend the next 32 years and your retirement fund to get the results I did. That's why I put this information together; to make it much easier and to give you the shortest, quickest, most effective way to Long-Lasting Happiness. It can be yours, in a very, very short time; possibly in the next few days!

If you can do three things, you can get more happiness!

I've simplified and laser-focused them; whittled them down to give you just the meat. Believe it: this information is enough to change your life—quickly.

Some people ask me if I'm perfect, do I do all the things I suggest in my books? Very funny. No way; I'm a human just like you. I have my moments, just figuring things out. However, I've had many successes on this incredible journey and I have been blessed with time, money, and the willingness to experience and experiment with different aspects of this amazing life on Planet Earth!

I give you a lot of kudos for investing in yourself and reading this book. It shows that you are above average, and have the desire and drive to want more true happiness from this amazing life.

Congratulations!

Big Tip: Mum's the word. I learned this a long time ago, makes you feel better in so many ways. When you are doing self-improvement things, don't tell a soul! Really, not even your life partner. I will tell you why. If you are doing something in order to improve yourself or help out others around you, if, for example, you only get to 50% of what you really were shooting for, you are the only one who will know you did not get to your goal, so there is nobody to beat you up. Others around you may think you're a Super Hero for that change!!! They did not know your intent was even more, so in their world you are even more amazing than before. So mum's the word!

So I've tried to be brief in line with the wise person who noted:

"If I'd had more time I would have written a shorter letter."

I don't think brevity implies lack of content.

> "Some of my greatest teachers were ministers,
> monks, and drunks."
>
> — *Jimmy Jerome Johnson*

CHAPTER 2

STUMBLING ON HAPPINESS
AND
WHAT IS A HAPPY LIFE?

HAPPY, Webster's says, is: feeling or showing pleasure or contentment, having a sense of trust and confidence in a person, arrangement, or situation. Satisfied with the quality or standard of; fortunate and convenient.

Origin: Middle English, in a sense, "lucky."

LIFE, Webster's says, is: the existence of an individual human being or animal, vitality, vigor, or energy.

For me, a happy life means feeling fortunate and lucky to be here, and experiencing this wonderful life on Planet Earth.

When I was 17 years old, in the summer time in California, my friends and I would go down to the river with inner tubes and little dime store inflatable rafts. We enjoyed ourselves immensely and life was a blast. On one particular day, my best friend's girlfriend and I went down the river in a very small inflatable raft, only to have our tiny little boat flipped over in some rough water. At first, we laughed and choked from all the water spraying around us. Then we started to realize our predicament and how serious it was; it was difficult to swim out. The harder we tried to swim to shore the more we were sucked under. We were in a water eddy, a swirling mass of current that has a lot of power. I did not know, at that moment, that Nancy had been swept down the river because I was so focused on getting myself to shore. I was so tired at one point I took a big breath, just relaxed for a few moments and started to sink! Then bingo, the eddy released its grip on me and spit me out. The current was still swift; however, I was not stuck in the eddy anymore so I was able to work my way slowly to the shore. When I got close enough, I grabbed the first little twig that I could use to pull myself to safety. Some strangers on the shore grabbed and pulled me out of the water. The only thing I could think about was Nancy at that point and so I quickly got back on my feet and ran down the side of the river. I saw her body floating and bobbing swiftly down the river. **OMG!** I just killed my best friend's girlfriend! Before I could get to her, some fisherman pulled her out of the water. When I got there, she was happily coughing, spitting up the turbid water.

What did I walk away with that summer? Three things. First, when all hell breaks loose, **take a big breath and just relax**. Second, I learned to **appreciate every moment** we have on this earth because it may be my last. Third thing: don't tell your parents you almost died! We never told them. I learned **not to focus on negative things or thoughts**; it would have just made our parents unhappy.

I'm going to show you the three main simple principle steps that will bring you more happiness now and allow you to maintain it. There are many other things that you can also do. I will discuss those later. However, let's stick to *The Basics*.

Depending on where you're at and your ability to implement the information, you can have tremendous results within the next twenty-four hours. If you are slow like I was, it may take the next three or four days. It will be difficult to go back to your old life. It will be undesirable. Imagine that!

I have spent many years in a foreign country where some people are poor and some people are very rich. From scruffy, wild-eyed lumberjack workers to police officers, the one thing they all have in common is they love to smile and think happy thoughts. It is part of their culture. The nickname for the country is "the land of smiles." Imagine that!

What is required of you to obtain this everlasting happy life? The first step is what you are already doing—you're reading this book. Kudos to you! Next, you need a little time every day; just a little, not too much. You'll also need focus; you simply need to focus on the self-talk, your thoughts, and learning how to redirect them. That's basically it.

So what does it take to have a life where you feel fortunate and lucky all the time? A little time committed to studying the three main principle steps. A few minutes a day and a little focus.

Have you ever noticed when you are happy for a period of time everything just seems to go so right and easy? When you're happy, you tend to bump into other happy people; it's like magic. When you're happy, everything just seems to come together for you! Now imagine having that happen every day!

I was on the New York City subway train, just standing and minding my own business. A young gentleman came up to me and asked me if he could get some. I was perplexed; get some what? The drugs that you are on, you look so...

Happy!

Life is good!

CHAPTER 3

IT'S JUST NOT POSSIBLE TO BE HAPPY MOST OF THE TIME! TEACHING OLD DOGS NEW TRICKS LOVE YOURSELF

Naysayers: some people will say, "The methods are just too easy," or "people really do not change," or "I have old habits, how can I change?" I'm here to say you can Do, Be, or Have anything you want. All it takes is focus in the right direction. What I've discovered in life is that the people who say it can't be done are the ones who take the easy road out, and complain, or do nothing, because they don't want to put the effort into making any real changes. I know that's not you because you would not be reading this book right now if it were.

Most of this stuff is very simple. However, there is some work involved, so you ought to focus and concentrate. It takes effective movements in the right direction to make changes. You may find this difficult at first. With a little progress every day, you will see vast improvements in a short time.

Some people say, "It's just not possible to be happy most of the time." For them, that is true; you are only going to get what you believe. I absolutely disagree with the naysayers. With a little bit of work on your part, you can do amazing things; literally, anything that you'd like—you just have to believe.

In my early 20s, the doctors diagnosed with me with bipolar disorder. I had up-and-down mood swings (which is basically synonymous with the condition). When I was up, the world was my oyster, and when I was down, my thoughts would spiral—it felt like the world was coming to an end. Some months, I would have one or two days when I could not even get out of bed; days when I did not want to hear the phone ring or talk to anybody. After a heartbreaking divorce, I decided to do it the doctors' way. They put me on drugs for life; the main doctor said I had a chemical imbalance in my body that could never be corrected. Once on the medication, I basically turned into a zombie, nearly drooling at the mouth. Wow! What an amazing experience; I was just an automaton. I was suffering from a huge lack of passion and drive. Then something wonderful happened! I met a spiritual man and he said these words to me:

"Everybody has emotional ups and downs in the month, some people just some have more of it."

Then he asked me an important question: "What did you do to combat these mood swings?" I told him if I got some exercise or at least went for a walk or called some of my positive friends to talk about upbeat stuff, that it would usually cheer me up. I went off the medication and signed up for a six day per week exercise class and made it a point to meet with friends weekly for fun! Bingo—that worked! Now it has been nearly 30 years with no doctors and no drugs; I've been living a healthy and happy life. I made a choice to use the power of my mind. I made a conscious choice and effort.

If I can overcome bipolar disorder, you can surely implement a few ideas and create a forever happy life.

You can Do, Be, or Have anything you want!

You can do this!

Life is good!

"The good life consists in deriving happiness by using your signature strengths every day in the main realms of living.

The meaningful life adds one more component: using these same strengths to forward knowledge, power, or goodness. A life that does this is pregnant with meaning, and if God comes at the end, such a life is sacred."

~ Martin Seligman from *Authentic Happiness*

CHAPTER 4

10% HAPPIER
NEW POSITIVE PSYCHOLOGY TRENDS

"At last, psychology gets serious about glee, fun, and happiness.
Martin Seligman has given us a gift—a practical map for the
perennial quest for a flourishing life."

~ Daniel Goleman, author of *Emotional Intelligence*
commenting on *Authentic Happiness*

"Happiness and well-being are the desired outcomes of
positive psychology"

~ Martin Seligman

In the 20 century most psychological research was focused on
mental illness. Many articles were published on mental illness
but only one out of 100 would be about mental health. Martin
Seligman was president of the American psychological Association
in 2000. He changed all that and made an aggressive approach
toward positive emotions and they call this new area "Positive
Psychology."

The main idea used to be taking somebody from a state of deep
depression to a medium depressive state to a zero, but the new
focus is on taking people from the flat line to very high positive
states.

It's pretty exciting to think that the scientific research today validates what other teachers and gurus have been saying for centuries—that valuing self-awareness, goal directed behavior, altruism, gratitude and other acts back up optimal living!

Common Virtues:

The writings and books of Aquinas, Aristotle, Bushido Samurai code, the Bhagavad-Gita and Confucius have the six things in common:

+ Courage

+ Justice

+ Love and humanity

+ Spirituality and transcendence

+ Temperance

+ Wisdom and knowledge

Strengths:

Don't spend a lot of time on your weaknesses. You're much better off developing your strengths. What are your five strengths?

1. _____

2. _____

3. _____

4. _____

5. _____

How are you using them every day?

1. _____

2. _____

3. _____

4. _____

5. _____

CHAPTER 5

HAPPINESS PROJECT DON'T COMPLAIN

Why not complain? You only get what you focus on. It took me a while to realize that. This is an important point. This is one of those things in life you must get if you truly want to be happy. For example, if you're complaining about something that's broken in your life, you're only going to get more broken things. It's the wrong direction.

How do I fix problems by not complaining? Okay, here's an example: you take your car in for repairs and they don't do the work 100% correctly. You simply point out how you would like it to be improved or corrected properly. The trick is to not to invest any energy into the situation. Do not get upset or frustrated. See what they say from their perspective, and be open to new ideas or new ways of finding a solution. Be happy knowing that it will eventually be corrected, and simply drop it from your mind.

If you find yourself creating negative mind-talk, you need to correct it right away. Think of the positive in each situation that you're in. As you understand that no person, situation, or event is perfect; it just does not exist. So look for the good things in that person, situation, or event. If that's difficult, just think of something else wonderful, and drop the negative mind-talk.

I'm the owner of a wonderful Apple Mac Book Pro. The reason I purchased it was to have less issues while traveling, as I spend a lot of time in other countries, some of them being Third World. At one point, I was having a major issue: the local Third World service department was causing me to pull out my hair. This obviously was not the same support I received from Apple in other countries. Then it dawned on me: I was so busy focusing on the problems that I was not appreciating all the wonderful benefits. As soon as I relaxed and focused on all the wonderful things about my computer, it was like magic. Soon I received a call from the service department in the next country over; they spoke perfect English, had parts and technicians willing, able and ready to take care of me. The universe will help you if you just allow it to. Focus on the good things and what you want.

Don't complain or you will just get more of what you don't want. If you have an issue with something or someone and you must talk about it, do it with no emotional attachment or energy. Stop the negative mind-talk in your head and change it to something positive (it can be a totally different subject).

You get what you focus on.

CHAPTER 6

THE BEST IN OTHERS
BEING YOU, AND CHANGING
THE WORLD

Even when they are drooling giant gobs of saliva on your jacket, train yourself to see the best in others. Look for their good qualities and attributes. This may take a little practice.

But some people I've met or known through the years are terrible. Do you have the habit of meeting up with some old friends, or maybe some new people, and focusing on their faults? Do you find yourself looking for their faults? Okay, I understand. Yes, I used to do the same thing. It's kind of crazy; in the United States, I believe we are born into a culture that inherently judges. Our parents, our schools, our government, corporate America—

even our churches; they teach us to dissect, to separate, and to put things in little categorized boxes. This is good, this is bad; this is too tall, this is too short; this is too sweet, this is too sour; she's beautiful, she's ugly. You get the point. Now focus on retraining your mind. Stop all this disempowering talk in your head. If you can't think of anything nice (in your head) to say about somebody, don't say it. You can always find something nice to say about something or someone if you have to say anything at all. "Boy, I sure like the color of her car," "He has a very nice hairstyle," or, as my wife says, without judgment, "Amazing." Sometimes, I'll simply say "incredible" and let them go on their way.

One of the many benefits to retraining your mind is it will free you up. It takes a lot of energy to be judgmental all the time. You will be freer and have more energy!

Just avoid the super bad, negative people of the world. If, for whatever reason, you must see these people, don't put any energy into the experience. Instead, put them in a positive light; they must have some aspiring quality to them, so look for that. And smile a lot.

A minister's daughter, a very caring and clever woman, was one of the top achievers in an MLM company I was involved with. She gave us an assignment. She showed us how to grow our business with some unlikely people. She told us to contact everybody we didn't like and let them know about our business. Yes, you heard that correctly: people who we did not like in our lives. It was amazing what happened. Some of the people actually thought it was wonderful that we cared enough to contact them. We had to find some good qualities about these people so we could tell them how they could benefit from doing business with us. So two things happened: Our businesses grew and we *'slew our dragons'* with people we had issues with (or we thought we had issues with). We also learned that all people are pretty much the same and have the same issues as us. People just have a tendency to judge others. Exercises like this make the world a better place. So, you too can focus on the best qualities of some of the least likely characters in your life story.

When you meet old and new friends, always look for the best in them. If you see your mind going toward negative things, change it; look for the positive attributes. If you have some super bad people in your life, simply be pleasant and smile; don't put any energy into it. That way, you do not carry any extra baggage around.

Finally, brothers, whatever is true, whatever is honorable, whatever is just, whatever is pure, whatever is lovely, whatever is commendable, if there is any excellence, if there is anything worthy of praise, think about these things.
– Philippians 4:8-9

CHAPTER 7

THANKFULNESS, GRATITUDE, AND APPRECIATION

Thankful: pleased and relieved

Gratitude: the quality of being thankful; readiness to show appreciation for and to return kindness

Appreciation: recognition and enjoyment of the good qualities of someone or something; a full understanding of the situation

As you can see above, both thankfulness and gratitude are two wonderful qualities to have. However, having true appreciation for something has much more value. By giving genuine appreciation for people, things, and situations, your life will be full of wonderful energy, which will keep you in the zone; a place that will fill you up.

The best time to do this is all the time, so make it a habit; retrain yourself.

When you see the self-talk coming on, or your mind start to take things for granted, simply focus on appreciation of that thing, person or place. It may take a little effort to retrain yourself.

Of the three traits (thankfulness, gratitude and appreciation), appreciation carries the most weight. When your mind starts to wander in a negative direction, simply turn it around and find good qualities in that situation. It's best to do this at all times—starting now.

I'm married to the happiest person on the planet!
She always has a smile on her face; I even have pictures of her smiling while she sleeps! I have only seen her sad once in her life that I know of, and that was my fault. What's her secret? Well, one of her secrets is that she looks straight into my eyes and gives me a heartfelt "Thank you." Thank you for this, thank you for that. She must do this more than fifty times a day. That's just to me; she must say it another fifty times to other people throughout the day! It's just her natural state of being, which was taught to her by her grandmother a long time ago; she was taught to be appreciative of everything in life, good or bad.
Everything!

CHAPTER 8

A CURIOUS MIND IN THE ZONE

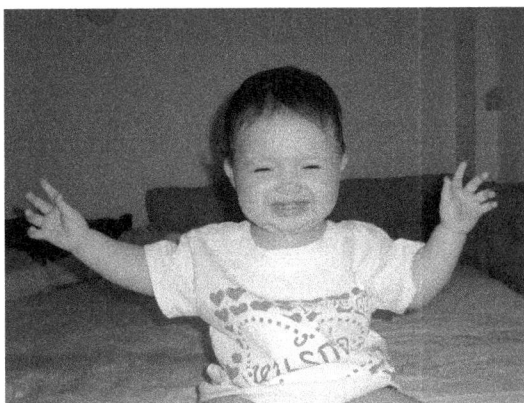

Zone: a state of such concentration that one is able to perform at a peak of one's physical or mental capabilities.

To get into the zone to which I'm referring, you want to see things in a positive light. You want to look for the best in all situations, people, and events; look for how they contribute to the well-being of the world and how they add value to others and yourself. This was covered in the last three chapters. When you do this constantly, you will see your energy change. When you start to complain, or focus on negative things, you will notice your energy changes also and you will be out of the zone. It's more difficult to create magic when you're out of the zone. It makes little difference how long you've been thinking negatively—you can retrain yourself starting right now.

This is a very simple concept, and relatively easy to implement. However, don't be fooled by the simplicity; this will radically change your life. Once you're in the zone, you will attract other things that are also in the zone to you. You will be happier and other happy people will be attracted to you; happy situations, fun, money, special circumstances, connections with others—lots of free-flowing joy.

I was in New York City with friends at our favorite Japanese sushi restaurant near Washington Square. The restaurant was packed, so you could feel the energy of the place amid the sounds of rumbling voices having conversations. People appeared to be friendly and happy. As one lady started to laugh, it was contagious. The whole restaurant started to laugh. When she stopped, everybody else stopped abruptly. That lasted for a split second. The second round of laughter made the place roar. The employees, the customers, the owners—everyone was laughing so hard we were nearly rolling on the floor. When you're in the zone, you will attract others to the zone as well.

In the depths of your being, you need to know and believe
that you are connected to your Creator's power.
You create your own reality with how you think!

CHAPTER 9

HAPPINESS IS A CHOICE
HEAVEN ON EARTH

Photo: Richard Sullivan

Happiness is a choice; you choose to have it or to avoid it.

Can it be that simple? If you choose, it can be. When you are mad, upset, irritable, or angry, think about where the feeling came from. That is a rhetorical question really; don't think about it too much. Actually, don't think about it all. You will just get more of that. It's better to focus on what you want, which is the good feeling you need to resolve the issue. Simply take a big, slow breath and consciously stop the behavior. Now focus on what you really want, or find a good feeling that will take you away from your negative emotions.

I lost 88% of my retirement money in this economy in a very short timeframe. I quickly realized that I had based some of my happiness on those investments. Did I become angry, mad, or upset with my brokers? You bet I did; I worked long and hard for that. One of the other investors who also lost a lot of his retirement money kept focusing and focusing on the issue, trying to figure out why he lost the money. While walking around and being angry, he wanted nothing more than to get even. Well, all of his focusing on the lost money lost him even more money and took quality time from his life. It made him even angrier and increasingly unhappy.

However, I realized that those things are not my source of true happiness. I made a conscious choice to look for all the benefits of what had happened. As a result, I've learned to invest my money in very different ways. I took a step back and realized something wonderful: my wife loved me even when we had little money. I learned to enjoy some of the simpler things in life. I have less material things to take care of and be concerned about. This also increased my focus when it comes to looking for all the great blessings and good feelings I have in my life.

Life is good!

Yes, it's just that simple.

CHAPTER 10

HEAD IN THE SAND
AND
POWER OF NEGATIVE THINKING

Some people would say to you that you're not seeing the real world. "With all the terrible things that happen every day, how can you just focus on all the good things? You have your head in the sand."

Yes, they are correct; there are many terrible things that are happening every day. There are atrocities that have happened in the past, and there are plenty happening right now. However, I want you to remember that you only get what you focus on. So, by focusing on these negative events, ask yourself: is that what you want for your life? The world would be a better place if we all focused on the good things in life.

Have you ever been focused on something so much that when you finished after a few days, or a few weeks, when you finish were surprised to see the world is still there? You were exhilarated from the experience! Now imagine having that feeling all of the time.

It is very important to understand that whatever you focus on, you get more of. It is totally your choice. Today there are many wars that have many nations up in arms against each other; people are killing each other, destroying countries, towns, and people's lives. Focusing on preparing for more war just creates more of the same thing; it's so obvious if you just look. If we would just open our eyes, we'd realize the solutions are easy and many. For example, stop using oil and put all the resources into creating a better world. Just for one moment, I want you to imagine we took all the resources for war and found a better way of creating energy. That would create many new jobs, the world would be more peaceful, there would be more real profit in the world to share, and we would be healthier and wiser.

The drug wars kill tens of thousands of people every year. We have created this monster killing machine to go after illegal drug dealers and drug manufacturers in far-off countries. Is this system working? Instead of fighting with force, why not focus on the smart solution? How do we take care of the people who want to buy the drugs? How can we help them get what they really want? They simply want to feel good, just like all the rest of us!

Whatever you focus on is what you get more of. So if you want more war and drug problems, focus on that. However, if you focus on feeling good, that energy will go out to the world and, in turn, create and attract similar energy.

"Smile and good things will happen, not the other way around!"

– Quote from a Korean Romance Flick, Almost Love

Life is good!

CHAPTER 11

LOVE, SEX AND FEELING GOOD

Do things, create things, and have things that make you feel good. You want to do this twenty-four hours a day; that equals happiness.

Is it that simple? Yes! If you don't believe it, I would suggest that, right now, you write down a list of good thoughts; things that make you feel good, for example.

Have you achieved major success at some point in your life? If you haven't yet, picture yourself doing and feeling it; if you have already, picture that wonderful time.

Toys: what playthings, gadgets do you own, had or want that can be fun? Some other favorite things you like to simply do, such as talking to a friend, having a cup of coffee with a friend, thinking of that next vacation, a new dress, a great meal, giving money to charity, having fun with friends or family, or a favorite time or moment in your life that puts a smile on your face. :)

These are just a few examples to get you going; you need to use ones more specific to yourself.

Okay, take a few minutes right now and make a list that you can use in the next exercise. Write down things, ideas, or concepts that make you feel good. Please do yourself a favor: get your pen and paper out and do your homework. Don't read the next chapter until you have done this exercise.

"The journey of 1000 miles begins with the first step."

– Ancient Chinese proverb

CHAPTER 12

SPONTANEOUS BENEFITS BY DESIGN

Photo: Richard Sullivan

These are few of the following things that you will notice immediately and some with more time.

+ More Energy: You will feel lighter with less baggage; hence, you will have more energy for creating! You can play and work for long hours without a thought.

+ Mental Clarity: You will think clearer. Sometimes, days seem like they have no end. You will be more present, more connected to others, nature, and the universe. You will be more in the moment, in the **NOW,** as Eckhart Tolle would say. You will notice things right in front of you that you did not before your new practice of Happiness.

+ Improved Relationships: You will notice your relationships with the people around you will change. You have changed; however, they will also change due to the positive energy that now flows out of you. You will also notice you are more attractive to others in many ways; your energy, physical body, and face, to name a few.

+ Offers: You will receive more love, sex, gifts, friends, business, and offers. You will rarely get sick, if at all. A good way to describe it is to remember when you were a child, and every moment was amazing; remember how summer school break lasted forever! There was always something new to do, discover, explore, feel, taste, and learn. When you breathed the air, you were sensitive to the smells and the moisture. Do you remember being Fully Alive as a child? What did that feel like?

The more you're in the zone, the more amazing things happen to you!

Life is Truly Good!

CHAPTER 13

SELF-KNOWLEDGE

Okay, it's time for you to make some real changes. Let's do an experiment; give it a whirl. For the next twenty-four hours, I want you to simply do the three things below.

1. Don't complain—about anything.

2. Seek out the best in others.

3. Have a great appreciation for whatever comes your way over the next twenty-four hours.

That is your assignment, please put the book down and see you tomorrow!

As Joseph Campbell says,

"Find your bliss."

CHAPTER 14

ASK AND YOU SHALL RECEIVE
HOW DO YOU FEEL NOW?

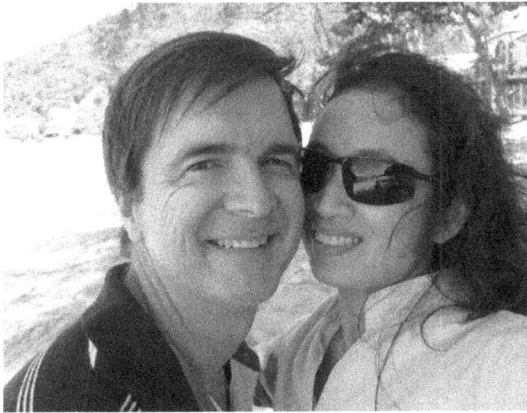

Okay, how did it go? **Feel better**? What happened? Was there a lot of work involved? Did you find yourself straying from the path? You've probably answered "Yes" to all of the above. Was it difficult at times? Was it worth it? Of course it was.

For some, this may be challenging at first, especially if you have never done any personal development work before. If that is you, don't beat yourself up. Take it slow and do what feels right and at what speed works for you. Remember, I had years to do this. I wish this book was around then. I could have had more playtime! For the rest of you, just focus and get better at the three principles. With time and a little effort, it will be natural and you will not have to think about it.

CHAPTER 15

PILLARS OF HABITS
SOLUTIONS
IN
MINUTES OR YEARS?

Huge changes can happen in your life in minutes if your intention and focus are in place. However, However, somethings may take years in a lifetime to get where you want to be What I've taught you in the first few chapters can happen in a matter of minutes. It's up to you if it sticks. You may need some practice.

This is your last chance. After this, there is no turning back.
You take the blue pill; the story ends, you wake up in your bed
and believe whatever you want to believe. You take the red pill;
you stay in Wonderland and I show you how deep the rabbit
hole goes.

Morpheus

I believe people who are truly happy continually want to create a better life for themselves. My belief is that one should never stop seeking the truth, improving and developing oneself.

A new habit/change/ritual can take time to sink in. Normally, it takes between 2 to 6 weeks to change an old habit or add a new one. After three months it becomes normal. I have found it's also very helpful to only make one or two major changes at a time. It's so important to get this point. In the past, after going to a workshop or reading the latest self-help book, sometimes I was so gung ho I tried to redo my whole life in one month, so many 'improvements'. So what happened? Actually I found myself at the Happy Hour bar after just a few days. :(

So pick one maybe two things that are the most important for you, new habits or rituals that will give you the greatest change toward the desires you want. And make them old hat, if they take a few weeks or three months is it worth it? Of course it is! Now build on this achievement and go to the next thing that you would like to add in your repertoire. It may appear that things are starting off slow and maybe that's so. However, the compounding effect will take over, and your life will make leaps and bounds. Truly magical things will happen to you, you will see.

One tiny little penny doubled every day for 30 days equals $5,368,709.12!

So that's it. It's very simple and you just need to follow through and be consistent every day.

This book was intentionally designed to give you just enough information to give you a happy life indefinitely. You really do not need any more than is in this book to see massive improvements. However, if you're like me you will constantly want to feed yourself good emotional, spiritual, mental food. So that's why I created a small series in bite-size pieces. So here you go... For even more helpful **Life Changing** tips, hints, and suggestions, download this book: *HAPPINESS LIFE, The Advanced book #2* from Amazon, which covers more than 20 other areas that can be of great benefit to you in your quest for an **even** happier life. Read the bonus chapter from the book just below.

Wishing you all the desires of your heart!

Jimmy J. Johnson

ABOUT THE AUTHOR

I was born Jimmy J. Johnson (JJ) in 1960 in the USA! I've worked, mostly for myself, starting at the age of 12 with lawn care and window cleaning. My dad was my supporter and inspiration for becoming an entrepreneur. I am proud to say I am self-taught.

At one point, I got up on a Sunday dead tired; I had to get to my dirty laundry, dirty apartment, and pay my bills. I had just worked another seventy-two-hour week, making someone else rich, and at that point, I realized it was not worth it. The amount of energy I spent to earn money and give me this lifestyle was simply not worth it. That was huge motivation for me to work for myself to find true Happiness, Money, Time, and Freedom.

Here are some of the companies I've started: E.M.I. (manufacturing of solar equipment), Xxellerator (backpack vacuums), and Small World Imports. I've had over 35 years' experience in the service industry. I've worked with some of the top companies who are the leading edge in cleaning technology.

At 47, I semi-retired and have built a wonderful home with my lovely wife and daughter in the Land of Smiles. I like to travel, and, as of this writing, I have visited 18 countries. I enjoy different cultures, food, and music.

NOTE: Many of the pictures in this book were taken locally!

"Life is an Adventure to be Enjoyed on a Daily basis."

– Jimmy J. Johnson

CHAPTER 4

THE HAPPINESS PROJECT

I have had moments of outrageous joy in my life. I was on top of the world, nothing could go wrong and all was well. Then other times it was just the opposite: the depths of despair, did not want to get out of bed, did not want to talk to anybody, and eating junk food. One pound bags of M&Ms were oh, so good! So I created a project to figure out why and how to achieve the good moments on a daily basis.

I read many self-improvement books on how to be a successful, better person and happy; many of them were hundreds of pages long, with complicated formulas, many steps and procedures to get you there.

Some things I found out before the happiness project. At first, I thought a lot of material things would make me happy. I worked hard and focused and bought a lot of fun material toys, and pleasurable things. I discovered if you're very attached to your things, they can just create more pain than pleasure—concern about things, insuring them, taking care of them and so on. Don't get me wrong, Material things can be so wonderful, and I have my toys. However, if something happens to them my world does not crumble, and my happiness does not depend on them.

Relationships:

Relationships and friendships, same thing applies. If you're attached to them, it can be very painful when people do not do what you expect of them, which is guaranteed 100% of the time. So the same goes. Don't be attached to your friends and lovers. Just appreciate them for who they are at this very moment, and take in the joy.

They will love you more for it.

Spiritual life:

I have studied and practiced many different types of religions, spiritual beliefs and practices. Unfortunately, many formal religions have so much dogma they have moved away from and choked out the simple message of truth. They can make it difficult to discover the truth. Everyone needs to find their truth for themselves. You must know and feel deep down inside that there is much more to this amazing universe we live in, and that you are eternal, and not just this body you carry around with you for a few short years.

I have worked and played in many Third World countries, for example Mexico, Guatemala, Costa Rica, Peru, Thailand, Laos and Malaysia just to name a few. I noticed that the people there have simple lives and simple pleasures and, for the most part, are happy. At first, I did not understand how they could be happy because most of them are financially poor. Then I discovered that they drew joy from their day-to-day activities, work, their time with family and friends, and not from what they had, what they owned, or controlled. Simple life, simple joy.

My wife was born and raised in a Third World country. Her grandmother taught her to be appreciative of everything in her life, to be happy with what you have, it was okay to desire things, however it was not to control you or make you feel happy or sad if you did or did not have these things. She is the happiest person on this planet that I know.

How to be happy all the time: It comes down to just one thing. It's what you're thinking about in this moment.

So, what you do is be mindful of what you're thinking about. If you're not as happy as you'd like to be, start thinking about something happier. Simply practice that and it will become a natural state of being in a short while.

When I started to watch what I was thinking, and redirected my thoughts to more happy and positive things, my life began to change. It took a little bit of effort and work on my part because I had a long history of finding faults in all things. However, as I focused on what I wanted and to feel better, things got better and better in my life. Wonderful people were attracted to me; business opportunities were presented to me.

Some days are like magic, wonderful things just happen.

For example, one day at the airport I was simply helping some people who could not speak much English with the airline counter person. Then later, when I was boarding my flight, to my surprise they redirected me to first class. Wow what a treat, that's part of the magic!

I retired at the age of 47 to an Asian tropical island paradise with all the time and money I needed, with no need to ever work another day, had true love, and friends around the globe. Two years later, I lost 88% of my retirement money in the market crash. To recover some of our losses, my wife and I went back to the United States, got regular jobs for low pay, drove a 22-year-old car and did not have much control over our work schedule. We worked 12 hour graveyard and 24 hour shifts in the medical field. Hard work. Basically, we worked day and night for one and a half years. At times we were dog-tired, however we were very happy. We were very happy because we used the simple principles in this book, focusing on the good things that we had, focusing on what made us feel good.

What did I discover in my happiness project? That material things, people, money, places do not give you happiness. They can help enhance it, however that's not the root of your happiness. What gives you happiness is exactly how you think at this moment. Not what happened before or what may happen in the future. You must think good, positive thoughts. Do the things that make you feel good. That is simple, but it will most likely take a little bit of work, effort and focus.

At one point I was working nearly 70 hours plus per week hard labor. I was in debt, broke, no money left over at the end of the month, drove a 14-year-old car and I rented a room from a friend to sleep at. No time for a girlfriend or friends. Basically, life sucked.

By changing the way I thought, implementing the ideas in this book series, the following changes occurred:

In just three short years I was working less than four hours per week, had time for friends and lovers, kayaking and sailing, was debt-free, Tithing, had a savings account, I drove a Mercedes-Benz *sedan and I was the proud owner of a classic Mercedes-Benz sports car (beautiful), also I had 10 acres for my 6000 ft.^{2} four bath, five car garage house and a brand-new rental home, three bedroom, two bath with two car garage.*

"If you think it is, life is good."

Enjoy the rest of this book and follow your joy to
HAPPINESS LIFE, The advanced book #2

Thank you so much for purchasing my little book. I really appreciate your positive reviews; they can be left at Amazon Click here :) I would like to make this book even better to help you and others move further on their journey to happiness.

Please send any comments or success stories to jimmyjeromejohnson@gmail.com.

One Last Thing:

When you turn the page, Kindle will give you the opportunity to rate this book (depending on what application you are reading this on) and share your thoughts on Facebook and Twitter. If you believe the book is worth sharing, would you take a few seconds to let your friends know about it? If it turns out to make a difference in their lives, they'll be forever grateful to you, just as I will.

Wishing you life changing success,

Jimmy J. Johnson

RECOMMENDED READS:

<u>Being You, Changing The World</u>

By <u>Dr. Dain Heer</u>   I devoured this! This is timely material and it's a must-read!

<u>The Four Agreements: A Practical Guide to Personal Freedom (A Toltec Wisdom Book)</u> Consciousness & thought, Native American, Spiritual

By <u>Don Miguel Ruiz</u>

<u>Better Than Before: Mastering the Habits of Our Everyday Lives</u> by Gretchen Rubin

Happiness, psychology & counseling, self-help

<u>How to Love (Mindful Essentials)</u>

by Thich Nhat Hanh and Jason DeAntonis

I always read everything by Thich Nhat Hanh

Happiness, personal growth & inspiration

<u>Self-Compassion: Stop Beating Yourself Up and Leave Insecurity Behind</u> by Kristin Neff   Timely new information

<u>The Power of Now: A Guide to Spiritual Enlightenment</u>

<u>Eckhart Tolle</u>   Personal growth and inspiration, motivational, education and reference. A modern classic already. A foundational must-read if you haven't read it yet

DREAM LIFE SERIES

RoyceCardiff
Publishing House

The purpose of this document is to educate and guide. The author does not warrant that the information contained within the document is free of omissions or errors and is fully complete. Furthermore, the author shall not have responsibility or liability to any entity or person as a result of any damage or loss alleged to be caused or caused indirectly or directly by this document.

The logos and names of other companies and products mentioned in this document are copyright and/or trademarks of their respective owners. Please respect their privacy as well as their copyright.